Hello!
I am a shark.

I0108788

Sharks don't have bones.

No bones about it!

Their skeletons are made of "cartilage".

Cartilage is what your nose and ears are made of.

Sharks have many rows of teeth that they can replace throughout their lives.

I bet I have (and lose) more teeth than you.

Sharks can go through thousands of teeth in a lifetime.

Cheeeeese!

A shark's sharp teeth point backward so prey can't escape.

Sharks swallow their prey whole or in large chunks.

I don't chew my food.

The fastest shark is the "shortfin mako".

I'm super speedy!

They can swim at speeds of up to 60 miles (97 km) per hour.

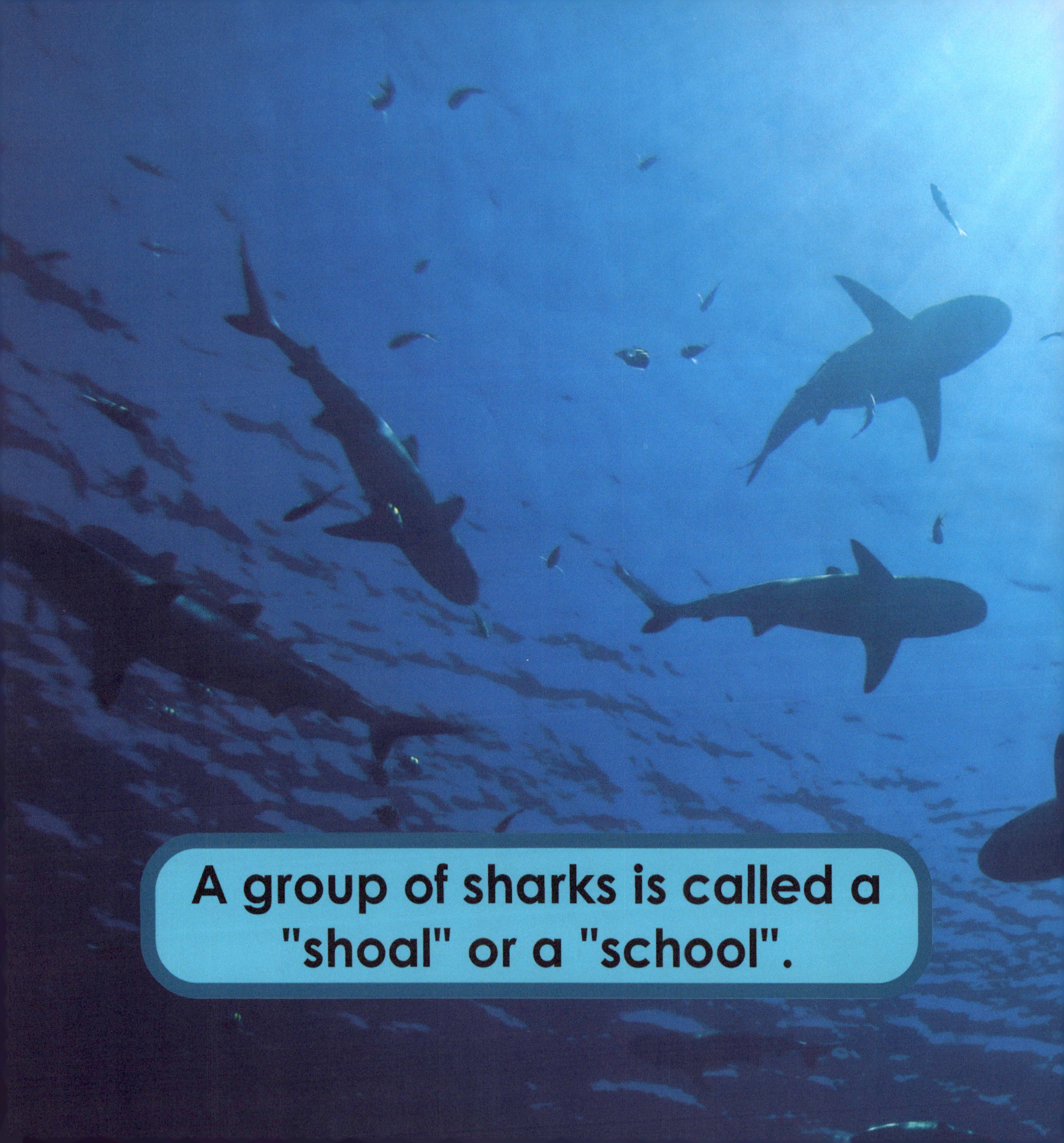

A group of sharks is called a "shoal" or a "school".

Baby sharks are called "pups".

Pups look just like adult sharks, only smaller.

I can take care of myself.

Shark pups are independent from the moment they are born.

Sharks can't stop swimming.

They need water to flow over their gills to breathe.

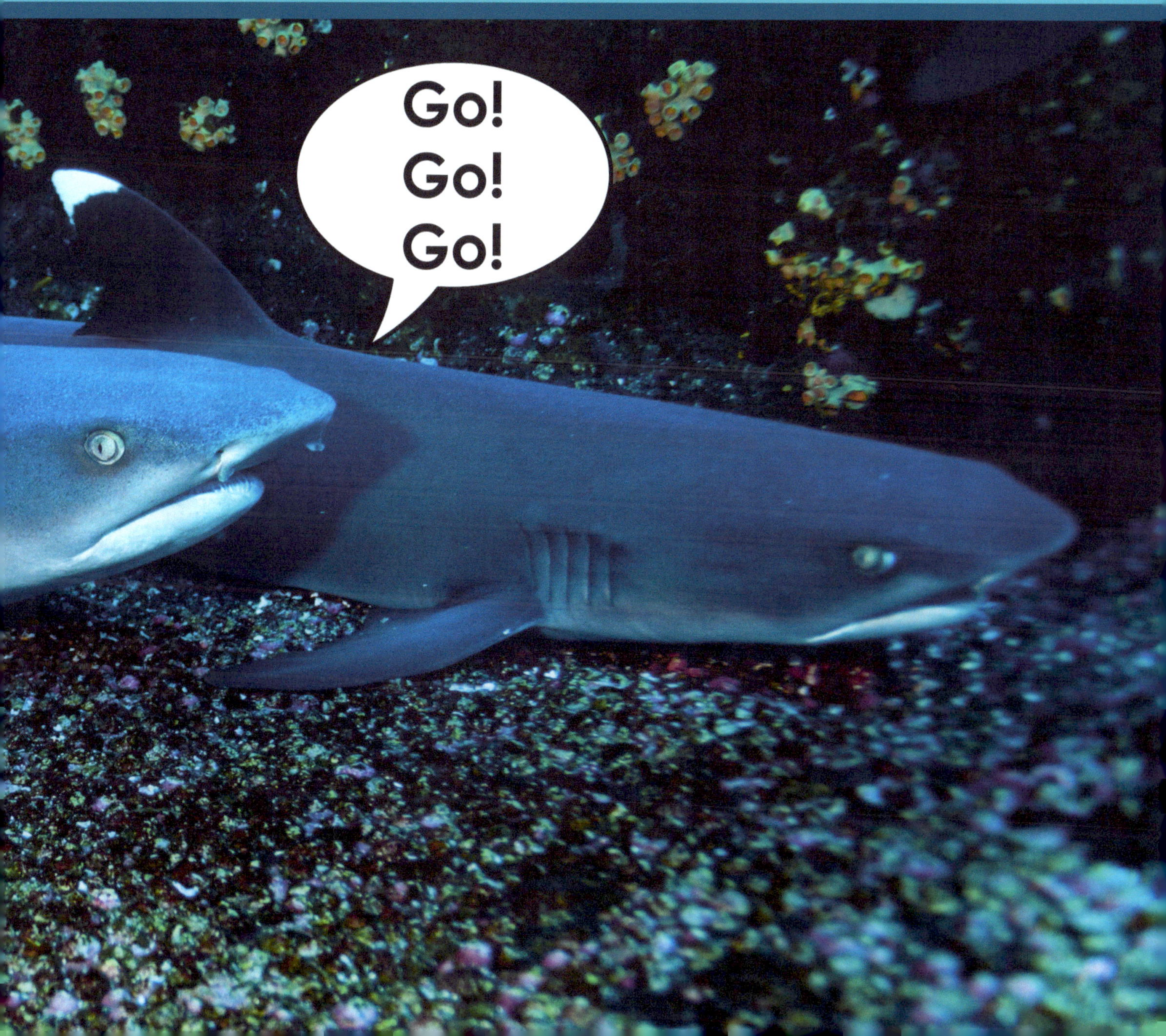

There are over 500 species of shark.

Sharks come in a variety of shapes, sizes and colors.

Some smaller shark species live for a short time. They may only live for 20-25 years.

Hurry up! There's not much time.

Some larger and more slow-growing species can live for 70 years or more.

Take it slow. We've got lots of time.

I'm the largest fish in the ocean.

Whale sharks can grow up to about 40 feet (12m) or more.

Whale sharks are "filter feeders". That means they mainly eat tiny plankton, small fish, and even small jellyfish.

I just swim with my mouth open when I'm hungry.

Sharks are essential for the health of coral reefs.

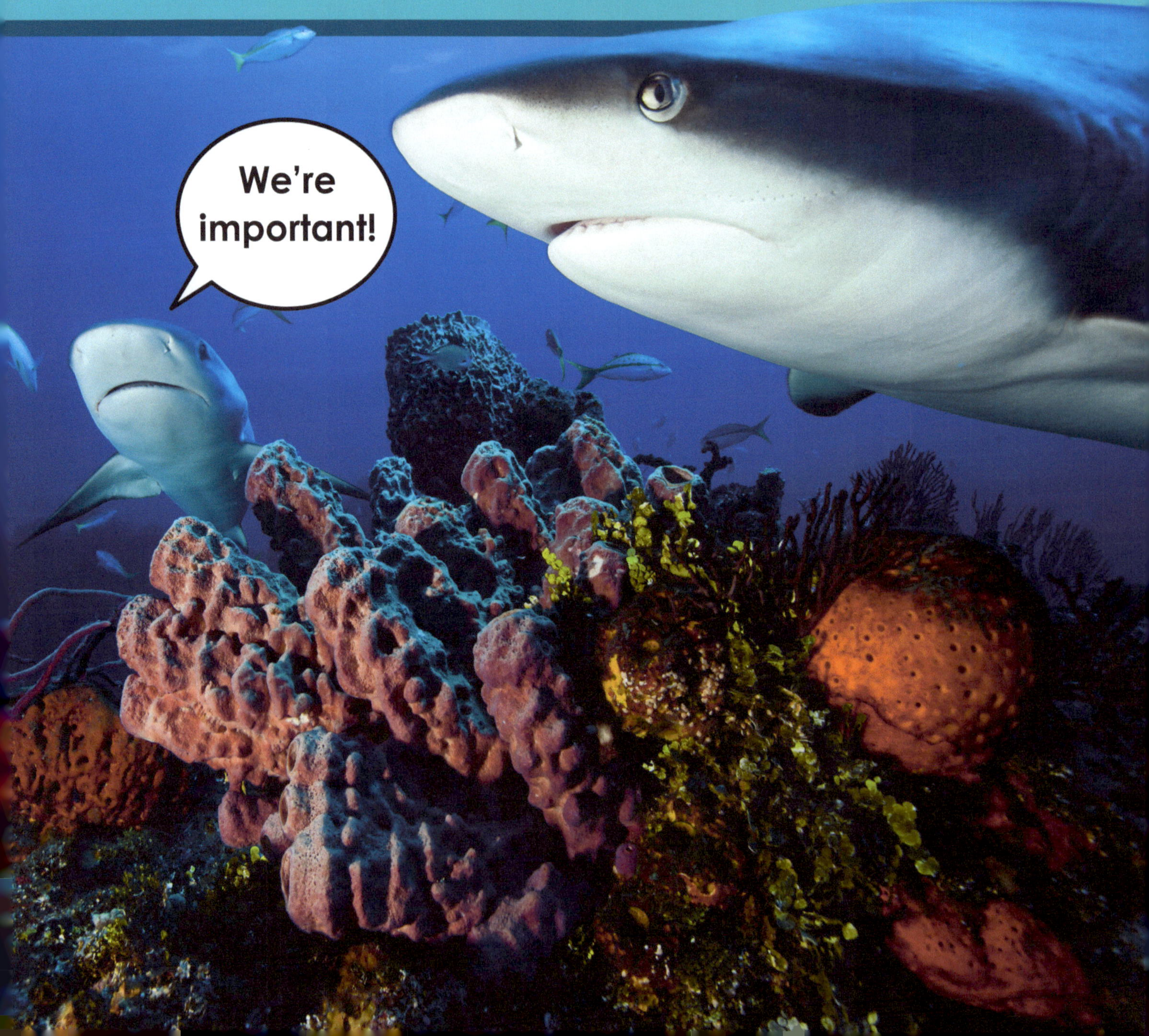

Some sharks can jump as high as their own body length to catch prey or escape danger.

Scientists believe that sharks might splash water to communicate with each other.

Look out!

Sharks have a powerful sense of smell.

I can detect tiny amounts of blood in the water with my nose.

Sharks can also sense electrical fields made by other animals in the water.

Speech bubble: We travel thousands of miles together.

Sharks often swim long distances together in groups to find food.

They also gather together in large groups to find mates.

Let's make a splash together!

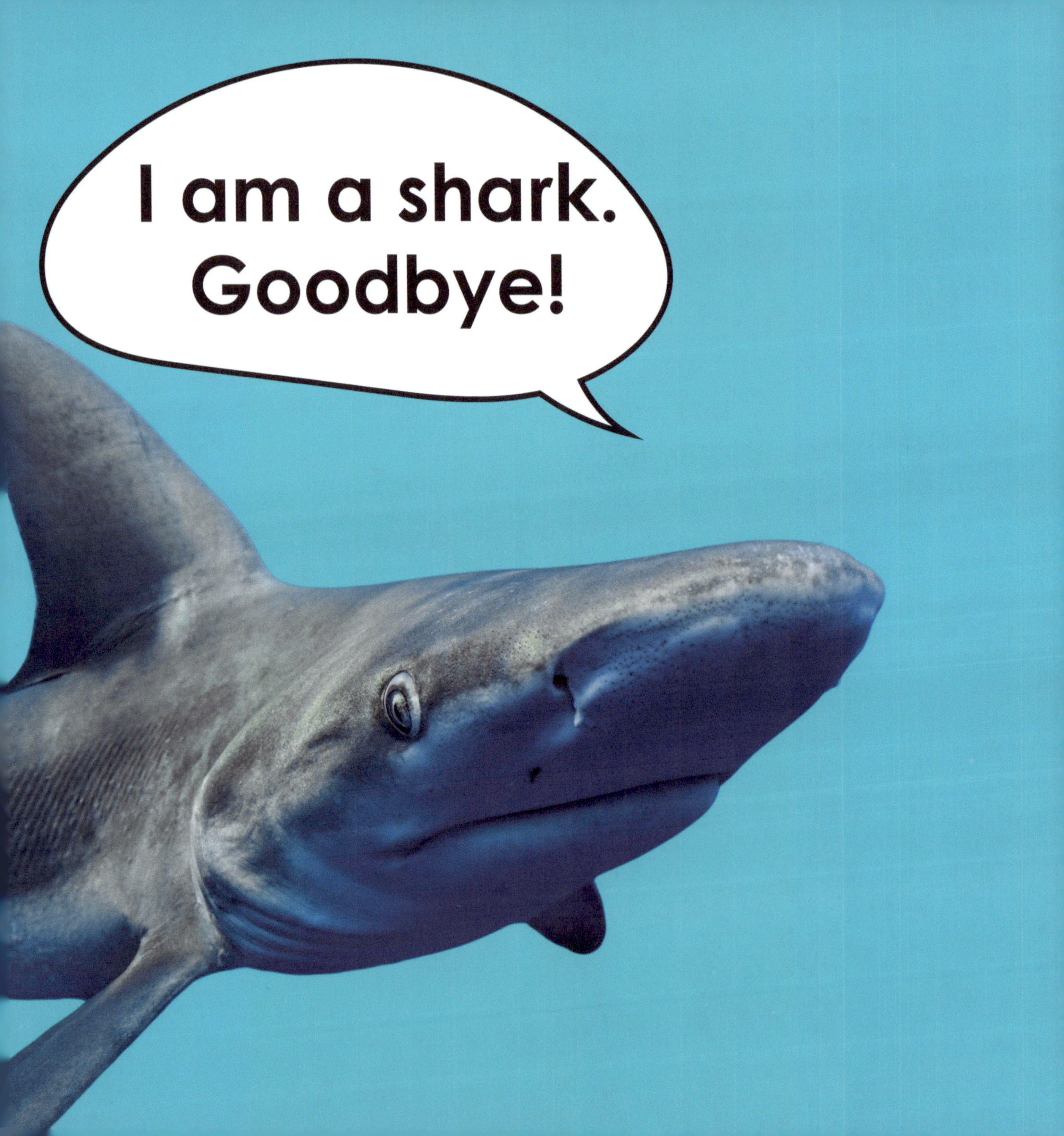
I am a shark.
Goodbye!

Want more?

... and more

COLLECT THEM ALL!
ActiveBrainsBooks.com

Hello parents!

Visit us to find out about new releases and **FREE** offers. We'll let you know when we have a new release coming out and how you can get it for FREE.
And you can cast your vote for what book we make next!

scan here

or visit here

ActiveBrainsBooks.com

---

scan here

Let us know what you think. As an independent publisher, your honest reviews mean a lot to us and our business. We'd love to hear from you!

amazon.com/review/create-review/

or visit here

FOLLOW US on Amazon.

amazon.com/author/activebrainsbooks

ActiveBrainsBooks.com

ACTIVE BRAINS

www.ingramcontent.com/pod-product-compliance
Lightning Source LLC
Chambersburg PA
CBHW042057040426

42447CB00003B/256